# It Isn't
# Always
# Easy

## But Always Know
## That I Care

Other books by

# Blue Mountain Press INC

**Come Into the Mountains, Dear Friend**
by Susan Polis Schutz

**I Want to Laugh, I Want to Cry**
by Susan Polis Schutz

**Peace Flows from the Sky**
by Susan Polis Schutz

**Someone Else to Love**
by Susan Polis Schutz

**I'm Not That Kind of Girl**
by Susan Polis Schutz

**Yours If You Ask**
by Susan Polis Schutz

**Love, Live and Share**
by Susan Polis Schutz

**Find Happiness in Everything You Do**
by Susan Polis Schutz

**The Language of Friendship**
**The Language of Love**
**The Language of Happiness**
**The Desiderata of Happiness**
by Max Ehrmann

**I Care About Your Happiness**
by Kahlil Gibran / Mary Haskell

**I Wish You Good Spaces**
Gordon Lightfoot

**We Are All Children Searching for Love**
by Leonard Nimoy

**Come Be with Me**
by Leonard Nimoy

**Creeds to Love and Live By**
**On the Wings of Friendship**
**You've Got a Friend**
Carole King

**With You There and Me Here**
**The Dawn of Friendship**
**Once Only**
by jonivan

**You and Me Against the World**
Paul Williams

**Words of Wisdom, Words of Praise**
**Reach Out for Your Dreams**
**I Promise You My Love**
**Thank You for Being My Parents**
**A Mother's Love**
**A Friend Forever**
**gentle freedom, gentle courage**
diane westlake

**You Are Always My Friend**
**When We Are Apart**
**It's Nice to Know Someone Like You**
by Peter McWilliams

**These Words Are for You**
by Leonard Nimoy

**My Sister, My Friend**
**I Keep Falling In Love With You**
**I Love You, Dad**
**Love Isn't Always Easy**
**Don't Ever Give Up Your Dreams**
**Thoughts of Love**
**Thoughts of You, My Friend**
**You Mean So Much to Me**

# It Isn't Always Easy

## But Always Know That I Care

Edited by Susan Polis Schutz

Blue Mountain Press™

Boulder, Colorado

Library of Congress Number: 82-70055
ISBN: 0-88396-173-3

Manufactured in the United States of America
First Printing: March, 1982.
Second Printing: April, 1982.
Third Printing: August, 1983.

The following works have previously appeared in Blue Mountain Arts publications:

"I will support you," by Susan Polis Schutz. Copyright © Continental Publications, 1979. "This life is yours," by Susan Polis Schutz. Copyright © Continental Publications, 1978. "If you know yourself well," by Susan Polis Schutz. Copyright © Stephen Schutz and Susan Polis Schutz, 1980. "It isn't always easy," by Laine Parsons. Copyright © Blue Mountain Arts, Inc., 1980. "It's easy to look on the bright side," by Jamie Delere; "If I could just be with you now," by Michael Rille; and "I feel inside of me," by Andrew Tawney. Copyright © Blue Mountain Arts, Inc., 1981. "I know it hasn't been easy," by Laine Parsons. Copyright © Blue Mountain Arts, Inc., 1982. All rights reserved.

Thanks to the Blue Mountain Arts creative staff, with special thanks to Douglas Pagels and Jody Cone.

ACKNOWLEDGMENTS appear on page 64.

**Blue Mountain Press** INC.

P.O. Box 4549, Boulder, Colorado 80306

# CONTENTS

There are times in every life
when we feel hurt or alone . . .
But I believe that these times
when we feel lost
and all around us seems
        to be falling apart
    are really bridges of growth.
We struggle and try to recapture
    the security of what was,
        but almost in spite of ourselves,
we emerge on the other side
with a new understanding,
        a new awareness,
        a new strength.
It is almost as though
    we must go through the pain
        and the struggle
        in order to grow
and reach new heights.

— Sue Mitchell

I know it hasn't been easy
for you lately,
and I can't even begin to tell you
how much you've been on my mind.
It isn't easy for me . . .
feeling so far away from you
when I want to be close enough
to hold you
and look at you
and to tell you
    with all my heart
that everything's going
to be alright.

— Laine Parsons

I'd like to capture a rainbow
and stick it in a big box
so that,
anytime you wanted to,
you could reach in and pull out
a piece of sunshine.

I'd like to build you a mountain
that you could call your very own
a place to find serenity
in those times when you
feel the need to be
closer to yourself . . .

I'd like to be the one
who's there with you when you're
lonely or troubled
or you just need
someone
to hold on to.
I'd like to do all this and more
to make your life happy.

But, sometimes,
it isn't easy to do
the things I would like to do
or give the things I would
like to give.

So . . . until I learn how to
catch rainbows and build mountains,
let me do for you that which I know best . . .

. . . Let me simply
         be your friend.

— Jacqueline J. Hancock

When the world closes in
and lies so heavily upon you . . .
remember that I care.
When the ones with whom you
share your life seem strangers . . .
remember that I care.
When love seems to only bring
you pain . . .
remember that I care.

What cannot be, cannot be.
But always remember, I care.
Never be afraid to come to me,
if you have need of the simplest thing.
No matter what it is . . .
      I care.

       — Kathy Carter Boss

If ever you need to talk,
    to share a laugh,
    a dream, a smile;
to be comforted
or reassured,
to be understood . . .

Remember,
my shoulder is there
    for your head,
your secrets are safe
and my door
is always open.

— Ronda Scott

I wish I could make your pain disappear;
   make your world right once more.

I wish I could say some magic word
   to make you feel happy again.

I wish I could give you a rainbow
   and make your tears go away.

I wish I could do so much more
   than just say:

   I am your friend and I am here
      if you need me.

                                    — Donna Wayland

I will support you
in all that you
do
I will help you
in all that you
need
I will share with you
in all that you
experience
I will encourage you
in all that you
try
I will understand you
in all that is in your
heart
I will love you
in all that you
are

— Susan Polis Schutz

There are periods of time
when things aren't going right—
times when all the plans you've made
might appear to be out of reach . . .
But as I have come to know,
the darkest and most difficult moments
actually signal the end of troubles
and forecast better days ahead.
From our saddest moments
we are able to gain strength,
    confidence and courage
and the knowledge that
a brighter day
is just over the horizon.

— E. Lori Milton

This life is yours
Take the power
to choose what you want to do
and do it well
Take the power
to love what you want in life
and love it honestly
Take the power
to walk in the forest
and be a part of nature
Take the power
to control your own life
No one else can do it for you
Take the power
to make your life happy

— Susan Polis Schutz

Everyone of us
experiences pains,
   loneliness or sadness.
We all deal with our inner struggles.
We all go through it,
yet so many of us
try to conceal the pain
and we walk around in
   even more sadness,
thinking no one understands.

But don't be so sad . . .
because someone does understand.
You're not alone.

— Jillien Cruse

Is there anything I can say
to make you not hurt so much?
I see you . . . upset,
and I feel it, too — deep inside.
I'm helpless, but
    I want so much to help.
Can I say anything,
        or do anything?
I wish I had the answers
            you need to hear.
I'm trying . . . but I guess that
the most I can offer for now
        is an ear to listen,
        and even more,
an open heart,
so you'll know that I care,
        and you'll know
        that I'm always here.

— Debbie Avery

There are times
when you have been hurt so badly
that you become certain
that the pain will never pass.

But it does . . .
sometimes because of your efforts
sometimes in spite of them,
but always,
   always it goes away.

So hold on, and know that
tomorrow will come,
and with each tomorrow
   it will be better.

— Sue Mitchell

## Making the Most of Life

The path to wisdom and success
   is not for kings alone; it is
   open to you and me.
You may not succeed at first,
but the failure of your efforts may be
the needed preparation for your final triumph.
If there are a hundred steps in your
      path to success
and you have not reached it in ninety-nine
      of them,
do not conclude that the journey is a failure.
Press on and up . . .
the prizes are generally at the end
      of an effort, not at its beginning . . .
and not to go on
is to miss them.
Be valiant . . . have faith in yourself.
Success belongs to him
      who dares to win it.

— George S. Forest

There is only one success—
to be able to spend your life
in your own way.

— Christopher Morley

Whatever the struggle
continue the climb
it may be only
one step to the summit

— diane westlake

As you move towards tomorrow,
may your heart be filled
    with a knowing and
    an understanding
of yourself and all that is
    happening around you.
As you feel one door closing,
    may you also feel others
    opening . . . just for you
And may you feel God's hand
    on your shoulder,
    in guidance and encouragement.
Know that you are loved.

— Rick Norman

There is no difficulty that enough love
will not conquer; No disease that enough
love will not heal; No door that enough love
will not open; No gulf that enough love will
not bridge; No wall that enough love will not
throw down; No sin that enough love
will not redeem . . .

It makes no difference how deeply
seated may be the trouble;
How hopeless the outlook; How muddled
the tangle; How great the mistake.
A sufficient realization of love will dissolve
it all . . . If you only could love enough you
would be the happiest and most powerful
being in the world . . .

— Emmet Fox

The journey of life takes us
through many times of happiness
and sadness.
We remember the happy times
as the most loved and enriching
experiences of all.
Although the sad times
do not outwardly appear to
benefit us,
they are,
in reality,
what builds strength and character
in all of us.

— Scott Palmer

You are equal to all others
some may have greater talents and power
where you are lacking
but you are greater in areas
      where they cannot go
do not stop your own growth and progression
by trying to emulate . . . or follow . . . anyone
step out with courage
develop all that you are meant to be
look for new experiences . . .
      meet new people

learn to add all new dimensions
to your present and future
you are one of a kind . . .
        equal to every other person
accept that fact
live it   use it   stand tall
in belief of who you are
reach for the highest accomplishment
touch it   grasp it
know it is within your ability
live to win in life
and you will

— diane westlake

You have powers you never dreamed of. You can do things you never thought you could do. There are no limitations in what you can do except the limitations in your own mind as to what you cannot do.

Don't think you cannot.

Think you can.

— Darwin P. Kingsley

Don't ever give up
          your dreams . . .
and never leave them behind.
Find them; make them yours,
and all through your life,
cherish them,
          and never let them go.

— Elisa Costanza

What is hurting
        you now
will come to pass . . .
patience is the gift that
            is needed
and an effort that
        is continuous.
Carry me with you
        as you go . . .
my hand is here,
my love is with you.

— Chris Bielat

When you're after more out of life;
when you're looking for the depth
and satisfaction few even know exist;
when you've got to do it your way;
and do it yourself, for yourself . . .

sometimes the disappointment
     is as deep
     as the joy.
The important thing to remember
is that the real satisfaction
is in the trying . . .
     and that I'm on your side.

— Dan Urbanski

God, give us grace
to accept with
SERENITY
the things that
cannot be changed,
COURAGE
to change the things
which should be changed,
and the
WISDOM
to distinguish
the one from the other.

— Reinhold Niebuhr

It's easy to look on the
   bright side of things
   when all is going well . . .
   when the smiles outweigh the frowns
   and the sunshine is streaming
      in the window—
But the happiest people
   are the ones who can say—
   when all is going wrong,
   when the clouds get in the way,
   that a little unhappiness
   .must balance the joys,
   and that a bit of sadness
   has its place in the world, too.

For they know, these special people,
   of the balance of nature's ways
   They know that nothing grows
   where the sun always shines,
   and that gray skies and rain
   can be an unregrettable
      sign of the day . . .

For these fortunate people,
   their favorite season
   is always the one they are in,
   and they continue to look
   on the bright side,
   knowing that the sunshine
         might leave for awhile,
   but that it will
   never be gone
   for long.

— Jamie Delere

It is a funny thing about life;
if you refuse to accept
anything but the best,
you very often get it.

— Somerset Maugham

Don't waste precious time
worrying about
what you should have done . . .
But rather, focus your attention
on what you are doing now,
and what you want to do
in the future
Don't concentrate
on any mistakes that might
        have been made,
but learn from them.

— Debbie Avery

Each of us
has far more courage
        and more "right" answers
        than we realize.
We can be so busy
focusing on our weaknesses
that we fail to see
        the tremendous capacity
        we have for carrying on.
Sometimes this courage is in the face
            of a particular crisis;
        but more than that
        it is there in all the small events
        that make up our everyday lives.

If we can just realize
how truly fantastic we are,
        we can approach the day
with the joys that we deserve.

— Sue Mitchell

Life presents opportunity—
     to live, to learn.
The world is ever-changing.
Finding opportunity in
   a changing world
is an individual matter.
The degree of living and
      learning
we wish to experience or enjoy
lies largely
within ourselves.

— Hiram Rasely

Although our lives
may not always be
      calm and contented,
remember to feel secure
with what you are . . .
feel stable
with what you can be.
Remain satisfied
that you are capable
of changing your life
      if necessary,
satisfied that you can try
and that you will succeed.

— jonivan

Have courage, and refuse to be defeated, and all will go well. You should know that you have the support of others . . . and if you look at the world around you, you will see that there is a new life ahead of you . . . one which offers wonderful opportunities.

— Paul Gauguin

I feel inside of me
the sadness in your heart
when things aren't going right

And my eyes, too
fill with tears —
because I know how you feel
and because I cherish you
so very much
and feel so close by your side

If only I could
I would right the wrongs
and make the days brighter;
because I want soon to see
the smile I remember
and the eyes that sparkle so
when things are going well . . .

All I have to offer
is my love . . .
>    to remind you that you're not alone
>    my hand . . .
>    to hold and to help
and my simple words . . .
>    that time will take you
>        to a brighter day,
>    and strength will walk beside you
>    and your heart will show the way.

— Andrew Tawney

The great thing
in this world
is not so much
where we are,
but in what direction
we are moving.

— Oliver Wendell Holmes

If you know yourself well
and have developed a sense
   of confidence
If you are honest with yourself
and honest with others
If you follow your heart
and adhere to your own truths
you are ready to share yourself
you are ready to set goals
you are ready to find happiness
And the more you love
and the more you give
and the more you feel
the more you will receive
from love
and the more you will receive
from life

— Susan Polis Schutz

# PROMISE YOURSELF

Promise yourself to be so strong that nothing can disturb your peace of mind. To talk health, happiness and prosperity to every person you meet. To make all your friends feel that there is something in them. To look at the sunny side of everything and make your optimism come true. To think only of the best, to work only for the best and expect only the best. To be just as enthusiastic about the success of others as you are about your own. To forget the mistakes of the past and press on to the greater achievements of the future. To wear a cheerful countenance at all times and give every living creature you meet a smile. To give so much time to the improvement of yourself that you have no time to criticize others. To be too large for worry, too noble for anger, too strong for fear and too happy to permit the presence of trouble.

— Christian D. Larson

We all have
   stumbling blocks . . .
what is most important
is turning them
into stepping stones.

— L. Kay Alexander

Though my heart's desire
   is to lift you over
   life's hard times

In reality
   I know
that I can only
   try to love you
   through them.

— Sheila Lance

If I could just be with you now,
I would hold you
and say that everything's going
        to be okay . . .
and you would know that I meant it,
        you'd be able to tell
by the meaning in my eyes
and the sincerity of my hand in yours.
And you would be able to know
how much I believe in you . . .
that you can make it through
any gray days ahead, because
I've seen you before . . .
shine so brightly from within.

— Michael Rille

Life is movement. We go up or down,
and develop the best or worst of us
in the journey. Some journeys are
full of struggle . . . some are full of success.
But the thing that makes for success
    is struggle and difficulty . . .
for without difficulties to overcome,
there would be no such thing as succeeding.

Difficulties develop strength,
    resolution, resources.
Problems are too often regarded as enemies,
    but they are not such.
Storms and dangers alone
                make skilled sailors.

The fiercest of foes develops your strength
    and your skill.
So do not be frightened by problems
    and difficulties—or discouraged
    because of them.
They are your opportunities
    for winning,
        your chances for success.

— Charles H. Parkhurst

Be comforted,
and don't be lonely.
The sun shines on you by day,
and the moon and the stars
   reflect their light
   on you by night;
thus are you loved
   by those around you,
with an unceasing, bright love.

Hold this love
in your hopes
   and remember it in your prayers.

— Joanne Domenech

One day at a time —
this is enough.
Do not look back
and grieve over the past,
for it is gone;
and do not be troubled
about the future,
for it has not yet come.
Live in the present,
and make it so beautiful
that it will be worth
remembering.

— Ida Scott Taylor

When you are hurting
   it is so hard to know
   that you are struggling . . .
I want to lift you up
   to a place of sunshine
   and mountaintops.
I know that sometimes
   the greatest gift I can give you
   is to leave you alone,
But when you need somebody,
      remember that
      I'll be there
      to lift you up.

— Sue Mitchell

It isn't always easy . . .
   this thing called life
Plans don't always work out
   the way they're supposed to
   and misfortune sometimes
   clouds the horizon
But . . . no matter how lonely
   the morning sun becomes
   we always have to remember that
It's up to us —
   we're the ones
   that have to push
   the clouds away

— Laine Parsons

# ACKNOWLEDGMENTS

We gratefully acknowledge the permission granted by the following authors, publishers and authors' representatives to reprint poems and excerpts from their publications.

Sue Mitchell for "There are times in every life," "There are times when you have been hurt," and "When you are hurting," by Sue Mitchell. Copyright © Sue Mitchell, 1981. And for "Each of us," by Sue Mitchell. Copyright © Sue Mitchell, 1982. All rights reserved. Reprinted by permission.

Jacqueline J. Hancock for "I'd like to capture a rainbow," by Jacqueline J. Hancock. Copyright © Jacqueline J. Hancock, 1982. All rights reserved. Reprinted by permission.

Kathy Carter Boss for "When the world closes in," by Kathy Carter Boss. Copyright © Kathy Carter Boss, 1982. All rights reserved. Reprinted by permission.

Ronda Scott for "If ever you need to talk," by Ronda Scott. Copyright © Ronda Scott, 1982. All rights reserved. Reprinted by permission.

Donna Wayland for "I wish I could make," by Donna Wayland. Copyright © Donna Wayland, 1982. All rights reserved. Reprinted by permission.

E. Lori Milton for "There are periods of time," by E. Lori Milton. Copyright © E. Lori Milton, 1982. All rights reserved. Reprinted by permission.

Jillien Cruse for "Everyone of us," by Jillien Cruse. Copyright © Jillien Cruse, 1982. All rights reserved. Reprinted by permission.

Debbie Avery for "Is there anything I can say," by Debbie Avery. Copyright © Debbie Avery, 1981. And for "Don't waste precious time," by Debbie Avery. Copyright © Debbie Avery, 1982. All rights reserved. Reprinted by permission.

Diane Westlake for "whatever the struggle," by Diane Westlake. Copyright © Diane Westlake, 1977. And for "you are equal to all others," by Diane Westlake. Copyright © Diane Westlake, 1980. All rights reserved. Reprinted by permission.

Rick Norman for "As you move towards tomorrow," by Rick Norman. Copyright © Rick Norman, 1982. All rights reserved. Reprinted by permission.

Scott Palmer for "The journey of life," by Scott Palmer. Copyright © Scott Palmer, 1981. All rights reserved. Reprinted by permission.

Elisa Costanza for "Don't ever give up," by Elisa Costanza. Copyright © Elisa Costanza, 1981. All rights reserved. Reprinted by permission.

Chris Bielat for "What is hurting you now," by Chris Bielat. Copyright © Chris Bielat, 1981. All rights reserved. Reprinted by permission.

Dan Urbanski for "When you're after more out of life," by Dan Urbanski. Copyright © Dan Urbanski, 1982. All rights reserved. Reprinted by permission.

jonivan for "Although our lives," by jonivan. Copyright © jonivan, 1982. All rights reserved. Reprinted by permission.

L. Kay Alexander for "We all have stumbling blocks," by L. Kay Alexander. Copyright © L. Kay Alexander, 1982. All rights reserved. Reprinted by permission.

Sheila Lance for "Though my heart's desire," by Sheila Lance. Copyright © Sheila Lance, 1982. All rights reserved. Reprinted by permission.

Joanne Domenech for "Be comforted and don't be lonely," by Joanne Domenech. Copyright © Joanne Domenech, 1982. All rights reserved. Reprinted by permission.

A careful effort has been made to trace the ownership of poems used in this anthology in order to obtain permission to reprint copyrighted material and to give proper credit to the copyright owners.

If any error or omission has occurred, it is completely inadvertent, and we would like to make corrections in future editions provided that written notification is made to the publisher: BLUE MOUNTAIN PRESS, INC., P.O. Box 4549, Boulder, Colorado 80306.